Addiction's Grip:
A FATHER'S STORY
OF LOSS

By
Armando Fuentes

copyrights

Dedication

In loving memory of my son, whose story lives on in these pages. I will always miss your fiery and witty personality.

Occasionally, your beautiful baby daughter inquires about "her daddy." I often remind her how much you love her and how you are in heaven watching over her.

This book is also dedicated to my entire family who endured this tragic and tormenting journey with me.

I also want to thank my close friends for being a comforting presence during my dark and worrisome moments. More importantly, I will forever appreciate the genuine affection shown to Alec when you opened your hearts, offering him temporary refuge and making him feel welcomed and part of the family.

Alec, the days we used to share are gone, but in my heart, you are always there; the gates of memories will always remain open. I love and miss you every day. You were on earth for a short period of time, but there is nothing more beautiful than a life fully lived. Your soul lives on the people you touched. Until we meet again, Love Papa!

Table of Contents

INTRODUCTION   1

CHAPTER 1 LIFE BEFORE TRAGEDY   2

-CHILDHOOD MEMORIES AND DREAMS: THE LEGACY OF MY LOST SON.   2
-BECOMING PARENTS AND THE JOY OF RAISING A FAMILY.   3
-MY SON'S EARLY YEARS AND PROMISING FUTURE.   4

CHAPTER 2 THE TRAGIC LOSS   6

-THE UNFORGETTABLE CALL   6
-DENIAL AND SHOCK   7
-ANGER AND GUILT   8
-DEPRESSION AND LONELINESS   8
-ACCEPTANCE AND HEALING   8

CHAPTER 3 THE LOSS OF ALEC (FUEGO)   10

-REMEMBERING HIS BRIGHT SPIRIT - THE DEVASTATING IMPACT OF HIS LOSS. 10

CHAPTER 4 DESCENT INTO DARKNESS   12

-WATCHING MY SON'S STRUGGLE WITH ADDICTION.   12
-THE HEARTBREAKING MOMENTS OF RELAPSE.   14
-COPING WITH UNIMAGINABLE GRIEVE.   20

CHAPTER 5 UNDERSTANDING FENTANYL OVERDOSES   21

-THE RISE OF FENTANYL.   21
-THE DEADLY EFFECTS OF FENTANYL.   22
-EXPLORING THE FENTANYL CRISIS.   24
-THE FENTANYL CRISIS: AN UNSEEN KILLER.   24
-OPEN BORDER POLICIES: FUELING THE FIRE.   25
-MY PERSONAL JOURNEY OF LOSS.   25

CHAPTER 6 OPEN BORDER POLICY   27

-THE CONTROVERSY SURROUNDING BORDER POLICIES   27
-EXAMINING THE IMPACT OF OPEN BORDERS.   28
-THE CONSEQUENCES OF INADEQUATE BORDER CONTROL   29

CHAPTER 7 DRUG TRAFFICKING AIDED BY THE OPEN SOUTHERN BORDER   31

-UNVEILING THE DRUG TRAFFICKING NETWORKS.   31
-THE ROLE OF SOUTHERN BORDER STATES IN DRUG TRANSPORTATION.   32
-THE URGENT NEED FOR COMPREHENSIVE BORDER POLICIES.   34
-THE INTERSECTION OF DRUG TRAFFICKING AND FENTANYL OVERDOSES.   34

CHAPTER 8 A CALL TO ACTION   37

-EMPOWERING PARENTS TO PROTECT THEIR CHILDREN.   37

CHAPTER 9 HEALING AND MOVING FORWARD   39

-THE JOURNEY OF HEALING.   39
-SUPPORTING OTHER FAMILIES AFFECTED BY FENTANYL OVERDOSES.   40
-UNDERSTANDING THE IMPACT.   40
-SUPPORTING GRIEVING FAMILIES.   40
-ACCESS TO MENTAL HEALTH SERVICES.   41
-ADVOCACY AND POLICY CHANGE.   41
-BUILDING A SUPPORT NETWORK.   41
-EMBRACING HOPE AND REBUILDING LIVES.   42
-CONCLUSION: JOURNEY OF RESILIENCE AND CHANGE.   43

$\mathscr{I}$ntroduction

Welcome to my book, specifically tailored for parents and teenagers who are seeking to understand the devastating consequences of fentanyl overdoses and the impact of this administration's open Southern border on the loss of my son. In the pages that follow, I will explore a heart-wrenching story that sheds light on the realities and dangers associated with drug abuse and flawed border policies. Through this narrative, I hope to raise awareness, promote dialogue, and ultimately inspire change.

Chapter 1
Life Before Tragedy

-Childhood Memories and Dreams: The Legacy of My Lost Son.

As parents, we are often reminded of the sweet innocence and boundless dreams that characterized our children's early years. Their laughter, curiosity, and endless energy filled our homes with joy and hope. But for those of us who have tragically lost a son to a fentanyl overdose, the memories of their childhood can be bittersweet.

My sons' childhood memories can offer solace in the midst of grief. They remind me of the love and joy that once permeated my home, providing a respite from the overwhelming darkness of loss. Reflecting on the happy times we shared with our children can bring a sense of comfort, allowing us to reconnect with their spirit and find renewed purpose in honoring their memory.

Furthermore, these memories can serve as a powerful tool to raise awareness about the dangers of fentanyl and other substances. By sharing my son's story and highlighting his dreams and aspirations, I hope to shed light on the devastating consequences of drug addiction. Through our collective efforts, I strive to prevent other families from experiencing the heart-wrenching pain I have endured.

As parents who have lost a child to fentanyl, I encourage others in similar circumstances to actively engage in preserving their sons' memories and dreams. Through storytelling, creating memorial foundations, or organizing events, we can keep their spirits alive while raising awareness about the dangers of fentanyl. By joining forces, we can work towards preventing further tragedies and offering support to parents who find themselves on the same painful journey.

In the face of immense grief, it is essential that we hold onto the memories of my son's childhood and the dreams they held dear. Let us unite as a community of parents who share a common bond and are determined to make a difference in their memory. Together, we can transform tragedy into a catalyst for change and ensure that no family has to endure the devastating loss I have experienced.

-Becoming Parents and the Joy of Raising a Family.

Parenthood is a remarkable journey filled with love, joy, and boundless possibilities. From the moment we hold our precious child in our arms for the first time, we embark on an incredible adventure of nurturing, guiding, and watching them grow into unique individuals. However, for those who have experienced the unimaginable tragedy of losing a child to fentanyl, this chapter aims to provide solace and hope, reminding you that despite the pain, the joy of raising a family can still be found.

When we become parents, we often envision a future filled with laughter, milestones, and shared memories. We dream of watching our child take their first steps, hearing their first words, and witnessing their accomplishments. Yet, life's unexpected twists and turns can shatter these dreams, leaving us devastated and searching for answers. Losing a child to fentanyl is an indescribable pain that no parent should ever have to endure. However, even in the midst of such heartbreak, there is hope.

While the pain of losing a child to fentanyl may never fully heal, I also acknowledge that it does not define the entirety of parenthood. Cherishing the memories of a child, honoring their legacy, and finding solace in the love and support of their family and friends can be healing.

-My Son's Early Years and Promising Future.

From the moment Alec entered this world, he was a beacon of joy and hope. His infectious laughter and curious nature brightened my days and filled my heart with immense pride. As a father, I watched him grow, overcome obstacles, and develop into a remarkable young man. Growing up in South Florida, we often enjoyed our beautiful beaches, theme parks, sports, family gatherings, fun vacations, and little league baseball games attended by the entire family.

Alec's promising future was evident from his early years. He possessed an insatiable thirst for knowledge, excelling academically and displaying a natural talent for creativity and problem-solving. He was smart with a determination and eagerness to learn, and I could not help but dream of the incredible achievements that awaited him; I often told him he should consider becoming an attorney.

As a young man, Alec's abilities in sports became apparent. He effortlessly mastered various athletic disciplines. As a little league pitcher, he had a strong, accurate arm. I couldn't be more proud and could already see him in the MLB. His dedication, discipline, and teamwork skills were exemplary, often receiving compliments from coaches for his pitching abilities and accomplishments on the mound, pitching a "No Hitter." I knew Alec could pursue sports should he wanted. He had a natural ability with good hand-eye coordination. I will never forget taking him golfing, naturally driving the golf ball without ever having formal lessons. I will always remember conversing with another golfer apparently impressed by Alec's abilities and stunt to learn he never took a formal lesson; the game just came naturally to him.

Despite his successes, I was not oblivious to the challenges that my son faced during his formative years. Peer pressure, societal expectations, and the desire for acceptance sometimes clouded his judgment. We had countless conversations about the dangers of substance abuse, but little did I know that fentanyl would become the tragic villain in my story.

Fentanyl, a potent synthetic opioid, infiltrated my son's life and shattered our dreams. The promising future I envisioned was stolen from us in the blink of an eye. The devastating consequences of fentanyl abuse are not exclusive to my family but rather a harrowing reality faced by countless parents worldwide.

Chapter 2
The Tragic Loss

-The Unforgettable Call

On the evening of August 22, 2022, under the warm South Florida sky, I gathered with loved ones at the local cigar lounge, a routine I cherished. Amid laughter and tobacco-scented air, a fateful call pierced the tranquility, heralding a life-altering moment. Little did I anticipate that the words spoken would plunge me into a parental nightmare, reshaping the course of my existence.

My loving son had fallen victim to a fentanyl overdose, a tragedy that has become all too common in recent years. The pain and shock were indescribable. We all have heard about this epidemic, read the harrowing news stories, and seen the devastating effects it had on families across the nation. But I never imagined that it would infiltrate my life, stealing away my precious son. As a father, I thought I had done everything in my power to protect Alec. I had instilled in him the values of work ethic, honesty, resilience, and the dangers of substance abuse. He would often reassure me and say, "Papa I don't have an addictive personality."

I thought he was prepared for any challenge that would confront him. Little did I know that addiction would sneak into our lives, disguising itself as a friend, a confidant, until it was too late. That fateful phone call shattered our dreams, our hopes, and our sense of security. It was a stark reminder that no family is immune to the clutches of addiction. I was plunged into a world filled with unimaginable pain, grief, and guilt. As parents, we blamed ourselves, endlessly questioning what we could have done differently. I have always been there for my son.

But amidst my pain and darkness, I found solace in sharing my story. I realized that I was not alone – there were countless parents out there who had experienced the same heartbreak, the same loss. By sharing my story, I embarked on a journey of healing, determined to turn my tragedy into a source of strength and inspiration for others.

Losing a child is a nightmare that no parent can prepare for. It is a crushing blow that shatters dreams, hopes, and aspirations. The pain cuts deep, leaving an indelible scar that never truly heals. The pain and grief that follow such a devastating loss can feel overwhelming and insurmountable. It is a reality that no parent should ever have to confront, but sadly, it has become all too common in today's society. The journey through grief is a rollercoaster ride filled with unpredictable twists and turns. The initial shock and disbelief give way to a deep sense of emptiness that engulfs every waking moment. The pain becomes physical, a constant ache in the gut that never subsides.

-Denial and Shock

The initial reaction to the news of your child's overdose can often be disbelief and shock. It is common to feel numb or disconnected from reality during this stage. Allow yourself to process these emotions, but try not to get stuck here. Seek support from loved ones, friends, or professional counselors who can help you navigate this difficult time.

-*Anger and Guilt*

As the reality of the loss sets in, it is natural to feel anger and guilt. You may find yourself questioning what you could have done differently or feeling angry at your child for succumbing to addiction. Remember that these emotions are a part of the grieving process, but do not let them consume you. Seek therapy or support groups where you can express your feelings and find solace in others who have faced similar experiences.

-*Depression and Loneliness*

Grief can often lead to feelings of profound sadness, depression, and loneliness. It is crucial to reach out for support during this stage. Surround yourself with understanding and compassionate individuals who can provide comfort and companionship. Consider joining a grief support group specifically tailored for parents who have lost a child to addiction.

-*Acceptance and Healing*

Over time, you may begin to find acceptance and healing. This does not mean forgetting your child or moving on, but rather finding a way to live with the pain and honor their memory. Engage in self-care activities such as exercise, meditation, or journaling to help process.

Remember, the grieving process is unique for each individual, and there is no right or wrong way to grieve. Be patient with yourself and allow yourself to feel the emotions that arise. Seek professional help if needed, as therapists and grief counselors can offer valuable guidance and support during this difficult journey.

While losing a child to fentanyl is an indescribable tragedy, it is possible to find moments of healing and peace amidst the pain. Reach out to others who have experienced similar losses, lean on your support network, and be gentle with yourself as you navigate the stages of mourning.

Chapter 3
The Loss of Alec (Fuego)

-Remembering His Bright Spirit - The Devastating Impact of His Loss.

Losing a child is an unimaginable pain that no parent should ever have to endure. In the devastating impact of his loss, I want to address parents and teenagers who have witnessed the devastating consequences of fentanyl overdoses and shed light on how our open Southern border contributed to the tragedy that befell my family.

My story entails the dreams and aspirations of a young life full of potential and promise. My beloved son, whose life was cut short by the deadly grip of fentanyl, became a victim of a system that failed to protect its citizens. I want to emphasize that my intention is not to assign blame but rather to raise awareness about the consequences of open border policies and the dangers they pose.

Fentanyl, a synthetic opioid, has ravaged communities across the nation, claiming countless lives. Alec, like many others, fell prey to this insidious drug, which entered our country with alarming ease through the wide open southern border. The devastating impact of his loss is a stark reminder of the urgent need for change.

Through my personal account, I aim to evoke empathy and understanding from parents and teenagers who may have experienced or witnessed the destructive power of fentanyl overdoses. We want to build a bridge of shared experiences, fostering a sense of community and solidarity.

I can tell you that the emotional aftermath of losing Alec has left a profound grief and anguish that accompany such a loss with ripple effects that reverberate through a family, a community, and a nation, leaving lasting scars.

My aim is not only to bring attention to the devastating impact of my loss but also to inspire positive change. I believe that by sharing my story, I can elevate the voices of parents and teenagers affected by fentanyl overdoses, fostering a sense of urgency to address the flaws in our border policies, and hopefully, we can elect the right people to effect positive changes.

In conclusion, the devastating impact of Alec's death is a painful reality that countless families face due to fentanyl overdoses. I hope to provide solace, awareness, and a call to action to parents, teenagers, and those affected by this administration's border policies. Together, we can transform heartbreak into hope and prevent further tragedies from befalling our communities.

Chapter 4
Descent into Darkness

-Watching My Son's Struggle with Addiction.

As parents, we often dream of our children's future, filled with happiness, success, and fulfillment. However, sometimes life takes unexpected turns, and we find ourselves facing unimaginable challenges. This is the story of Alec's battle with addiction, specifically, his tragic overdose of fentanyl.

Addiction is an insidious disease that can transform our beloved children into unrecognizable versions of themselves. My son was once a vibrant and promising young man, but addiction slowly took hold of his life, leading him down a dark and treacherous path. I watched helplessly as he spiraled deeper into the clutches of this merciless demon.

The journey of addiction is often fraught with heartbreak, confusion, and despair. We, as parents, experienced a rollercoaster of emotions, ranging from denial to anger to overwhelming grief. We questioned ourselves, wondering if we had missed any signs or failed to offer the necessary support.

Fentanyl, a potent synthetic opioid, played a significant role in my son's tragic demise. It is crucial for parents to understand the dangers of this lethal substance and be aware of its prevalence in the illicit drug market. Fentanyl is often disguised as other drugs, making it even more challenging to detect. Educating ourselves about fentanyl and its devastating consequences is crucial to protect our children from its deadly grip.

One of the most challenging aspects of watching Alec battle addiction was the constant struggle between enabling and tough love. I grappled with our desire to help him while simultaneously understanding that enabling his destructive behavior would only prolong his suffering. This delicate balance required immense strength, self-reflection, and seeking guidance from addiction specialists and support groups.

As parents, it is essential to prioritize self-care while navigating the harrowing journey of addiction. The weight of my son's struggle can easily consume my life, threatening my mental and physical well-being. Seeking therapy, finding solace in support groups, and maintaining healthy boundaries become crucial steps in preserving my own resilience and strength.

Ultimately, my story serves as a reminder to all parents who have experienced the devastating loss of a child to fentanyl or any other substance. We are not alone in our grief, and through sharing our experiences, we can find solace and support in others who have walked similar paths.

While we cannot change the past, we can honor our children's memories by advocating for addiction awareness, supporting organizations dedicated to addiction recovery, and ensuring that other parents are equipped with the knowledge and resources to protect their own children.

Remember, as parents, we are not defined by our children's struggles or their tragic ends. Rather, we can find strength in our shared experiences and use our voices to bring about change and prevent other families from enduring the same heartache. Together, we can make a difference.

-*The Heartbreaking Moments of Relapse.*

Frankly, I lived with the constant fear that someday the unimaginable would occur.

The heartbreaking moments of relapse can be some of the most challenging and devastating experiences for parents who have lost a child to a fentanyl overdose. For parents who have lost a child to fentanyl, the hope of recovery can be a flickering candle in the darkness, especially when very few make a full recovery. Addiction is a lifelong disease that doesn't go away, and fighting this battle means staying away from all substances. When my son battled addiction and managed to overcome it, there was a glimmer of optimism that life could return to some semblance of normalcy. However, the reality is far from simple. The constant fear of relapse looms overhead like a dark cloud, threatening to shatter any sense of stability. Alec once shared with me how he began experimenting with marijuana in middle school, despite our multiple conversations to stay away from all drugs. I was oblivious to this because I never witnessed him impaired in any way. In subsequent conversations, he also admitted to experimenting with harder drugs during his high school years, including opioids.

Despite attending several private drug rehabilitation facilities, he would revert back to using drugs, at times causing me to utter harsh words towards him, not for lack of love but out of anger and desperation, which I apologized for; I simply wanted to help Alec get rid of this daemon taking control and destroying his entire life. I realized it wasn't that simple, and he was facing a serious problem that only he could fix. A very good friend told me that "once you are on that train, it is merely impossible to get off." Alec was the only person that could request help.

When the heartbreaking moment of relapse occurs, parents often find themselves caught between conflicting emotions. There is the overwhelming sadness and disappointment that their child has succumbed to the grips of addiction once again. Yet, there is also a deep understanding that addiction is a disease, and relapse is a part of the recovery process for many individuals. It is a painful paradox that parents must grapple with as they try to balance their love for their child with the frustration and heartache of relapse.

In these moments, parents may find themselves questioning their own actions and decisions. They may wonder if there was something more they could have done to prevent the relapse, if they missed any warning signs or if they simply failed as parents. These thoughts can consume their minds, adding a heavy burden to an already overwhelming grief.

Support networks become vital during these heartbreaking moments. Connecting with other parents who have faced similar tragedies can provide a sense of understanding and solidarity. Sharing stories, experiences, and coping mechanisms can be cathartic, helping parents navigate the complex emotions they are experiencing.

While relapse can seem like a devastating setback, it is essential for parents to remember that recovery is not a linear process. Each step forward and backward is a part of the journey. By supporting their child with empathy, love, and access to professional help, parents can continue to be a source of strength and hope.

In conclusion, the heartbreaking moments of relapse are a painful reality for parents who have lost a child to a fentanyl overdose. Navigating the emotional rollercoaster of disappointment, guilt, and grief can be incredibly challenging. However, by seeking support and understanding, parents can find solace in knowing that they are not alone in their struggles. The journey of recovery is complex, and relapse should be viewed as a part of the process rather than a failure. Together, parents can continue to support their children and work towards healing.

Alec would tell me, "I know you're not my biggest fan." I'd shoot back, assuring him that it couldn't be further from the truth— I loved him to bits. It's just that seeing him in his current state tore me up inside. He understood the hurt I was feeling, but those darn drugs had this relentless grip on his soul, messing with his ability to make clear-headed decisions.

Despite how angry I felt, I would remind him of how the entire family loved him and wanted to see him healthy and free from all substances. We were all hopeful that he would find the help and strength to fight the daemon that had taken over his life.

Alec had become a totally different person; his demeanor completely changed, and he became disrespectful towards me and family members. He was very careless and didn't care. He was just out of control. A couple of weeks prior to his death, he took his mother's new car in the middle of the night without her permission and drove it into a nearby wooded area after falling asleep behind the wheel. Alec survived that accident without any major injuries, sustaining several scratches and bruises. Thank god he did not come in contact with any other vehicle. This was just another example of his poor decision-making and carelessness towards the end of his life. I am to assume he was probably high and nodded off, causing him to veer off the road.

Alec's vibrant spirit earned him the nickname "Fuego" among his friends, a testament to his fiery persona. Adored by many, he found a special place in the heart of his best friend, Zach. In a touching display of affection, Zach immortalized Alec's essence through a mural, a vivid reflection of their teenage camaraderie.

The memories of those carefree days, just a couple of teenagers having a blast, linger in my mind. Yet, in an inexplicable instant, Alec was gone—shocking, devastating, and utterly unimaginable. The same flame that once ignited our hearts, a beacon of light in our lives, was cruelly extinguished by the deadly grip of fentanyl, a culprit responsible for claiming the lives of 80,000 people a year.

Just two days after the car accident, Alec was gone. His mom noticed something was off when he didn't come upstairs to say goodbye to his daughter Kylie before school, like he always did. When she got back from work, she went to check on him. Going down the stairs, she felt a sense of worry. Turning the corner, she found Alec lifeless on the floor next to his office chair.

On his desk, there was a small plastic bag with some white powder substance inside. It was a harsh reminder of Alec's struggle with drugs. As his mom got closer, it was clear he had been gone for a while. She described him as cold to the touch, with his skin showing a strange purplish-red color due to something called Livor mortis. It was a sad and tough moment, realizing the grip of addiction had taken Alec away.

Receiving that devastating call, my mind couldn't help but wander to the unimaginable scene Kim confronted, finding Alec alone. My heart ached for her. I envisioned the emotional storm she must have weathered – shock, disbelief, confusion, horror, and fear crashing down on her all at once.

In those agonizing moments, Kim faced this heart-wrenching reality all on her own, with only her love for Kylie to anchor her. The weight of having to shield Alec's daughter from witnessing him in such a state must have been crushing. She navigated the chaos of first responders and government officials descending on the scene, all while grappling with the surreal nightmare unfolding around her. The strength she summoned in that desolate moment is a testament to a mother's resilience in the face of unspeakable tragedy.

I was fortunate to be surrounded by family when I was notified of this terrible and unforgettable news.

By the time the first responders arrived at the house, Alec had already been gone for some time. An autopsy and toxicology were ordered, revealing his cause of death as acute fentanyl intoxication, and the manner of death was ruled as accidental leaving this world at only 25 years old.

In my interactions with Alec, I could see changes like depression, anxiety, reduced motivation, difficulties experiencing pleasure, apathy, and even more serious symptoms, such as the development of hallucinations at times.

For those of us who have tragically lost a son to a fentanyl overdose, the memories of their childhood can be bittersweet. I was beyond upset at my son. I never thought he would be dealing with addiction, especially growing up in a home free of drugs and alcohol; notwithstanding being a former South Florida detective, I felt betrayed by my own son. Alec knew how hurt and distant we became, as we had little in common.

No one is allowed in the mind of a person with addiction except for them. They are the only ones who can decide to change their lives, for better or for worse. This will not end until they decide to end it. Many times, parents try to make that decision for them, and it only winds up resulting in more frustration and failure; I know that firsthand with Alec. What parents can do is encourage them to seek help and treatment and let them arrive at the decision themselves. Subject experts I have spoken with mentioned that a good amount of individuals relapse within 30 days of leaving an inpatient drug and alcohol treatment center. It is important for individuals who struggle with substance addiction to acknowledge the high risk for relapse, have an awareness of what their own personal triggers are, and learn to cope with their triggers and emotions in a healthy way.

Border officials seized 4,600 pounds of fentanyl along the southern border in 2020, a number that skyrocketed to 26,700 pounds in FY 2023 – a 480 percent increase. Most of the fentanyl seized by the two agencies in FY 2023, about 98.9 percent (26,700 out of 27,000 pounds), was seized at the southern border.

This current administration ignited the worst border crisis in American history and placed U.S. Border Patrol agents' lives at risk by removing deterrent-focused immigration policies and border enforcement tools.

As parents, we are constantly worried about the safety and well-being of our children. We do everything in our power to protect them from harm, to guide them through life's challenges, and to ensure their future is bright. But what happens when an unexpected tragedy strikes, leaving us shattered and questioning the very policies that were meant to protect us?

Through my research and conversations with experts, I learned that the lax enforcement and porous borders in the Southern region had inadvertently created a gateway for the illegal trafficking of drugs like never before. Fentanyl, a potent and highly addictive opioid, is pouring into our country at an alarming rate, claiming countless lives and tearing families apart. We were left wondering how such a tragedy could have been prevented and why our government had not taken decisive action to address this crisis.

-Coping with Unimaginable Grieve.

Losing a child is an unimaginable tragedy that no parent should ever have to endure. The pain and grief that accompanies such a loss can be overwhelming, leaving parents feeling helpless and lost.

For parents who have lost a child to fentanyl overdose, the pain is compounded by the knowledge our open Southern border played in their child's untimely demise. The grief they experience is not only a personal loss but also a larger reflection of the failures within the system that allowed dangerous substances to flow freely across borders.

Chapter 5
Understanding Fentanyl Overdoses

-The Rise of Fentanyl.

In recent years, there has been a dramatic increase in the use and abuse of a highly potent synthetic opioid called fentanyl. This deadly drug has become a major concern for parents, teenagers, and communities across the nation. Its rise can be attributed to a variety of factors, including the consequences of our open Southern border policies. As a parent who has experienced the devastating loss of a child due to a fentanyl overdose, I feel compelled to shed light on this pressing issue.

Fentanyl is a synthetic opioid that is up to 50 times more potent than heroin and 100 times more potent than morphine. Originally developed for medical use, it has found its way into the illicit drug market, where it is often mixed with other substances like heroin or cocaine, amplifying its lethal effects. The accessibility and affordability of fentanyl have made it an attractive option for drug dealers, leading to a surge in its distribution and consumption.

One of the key factors contributing to the rise of fentanyl is the porous Southern border. The lax border policies have allowed drug cartels and criminal organizations to smuggle vast quantities of fentanyl into the United States. These groups take advantage of the loopholes and lack of effective border control measures to transport this deadly drug across the border undetected.

Tragically, Alec fell victim to this epidemic. Like many teenagers, he was enticed by the allure of experimentation and peer pressure.

It is crucial for parents and teenagers to be aware of the dangers posed by fentanyl. Education and open conversations about the risks associated with drug abuse can help prevent further tragedies. Recognizing the signs of fentanyl use, such as constricted pupils, slowed breathing, and extreme drowsiness is vital in identifying potential cases of overdose.

Furthermore, it is imperative that we address the root causes of the fentanyl crisis. Strengthening border security and implementing stricter regulations on the importation of synthetic drugs are essential steps in curbing the flow of fentanyl into our communities. By holding accountable those responsible for its distribution, we can protect our children from falling victim to this deadly substance.

The rise of fentanyl is a stark reminder of the devastating consequences of wide open Southern border policies. As parents, it is our duty to advocate for change and ensure the safety and well-being of our children. By raising awareness, fostering dialogue, and demanding action, we can transform heartbreak into hope and prevent the future loss of innocent lives.

-The Deadly Effects of Fentanyl.

Fentanyl, a synthetic opioid, has become one of the deadliest drugs in recent years, causing an alarming rise in fatal overdoses across the United States. This subchapter aims to shed light on the devastating consequences of fentanyl use, particularly concerning our wide-open Southern border that has contributed to its widespread availability. Addressing parents and teenagers alike, it serves as a cautionary tale and a wake-up call to the dangers lurking behind this deadly drug.

Fentanyl, touted as a painkiller, is approximately 50-100 times more potent than morphine. Its immense strength makes it a popular choice for drug dealers and manufacturers to cut other illicit substances, such as heroin or cocaine, resulting in a lethal combination. The consequences of this lethal mix have been catastrophic, leading to an unprecedented surge in fentanyl-related overdoses.

Our invisible Southern border has inadvertently facilitated the smuggling of fentanyl into the country. Criminal organizations exploit these porous borders, taking advantage of the lax security measures to transport large quantities of this deadly drug. As a result, fentanyl has flooded our streets, claiming countless lives and tearing apart families.

Many parents have had to endure the heartbreak of losing their children to fentanyl overdoses.

To combat the deadly effects of fentanyl, it is crucial to educate both parents and teenagers about the risks associated with its use. Parents need to be aware of the signs of fentanyl abuse and be equipped with the knowledge to start conversations with their children about the dangers of experimenting with drugs. Teenagers, on the other hand, must understand the potentially lethal consequences of even a single encounter with fentanyl.

I aim to raise awareness and ignite a sense of urgency among parents and teenagers alike. It is a call to action, urging parents to advocate for stricter border policies and demanding that authorities take decisive measures to combat the fentanyl crisis. By coming together as a community, we can prevent further heartbreak and loss and pave the way for hope and a safer future for our children.

-Exploring the Fentanyl Crisis.

The Fentanyl Crisis: A Grave Concern for Parents and Teenagers.

I delve into the heart-wrenching reality of the fentanyl crisis, a growing epidemic that has affected countless lives. As parents, it is our duty to protect and guide our teenagers, and understanding the dangers of fentanyl overdoses is crucial in safeguarding their futures. I will also explore the role our wide open Southern border has played in exacerbating this crisis as I share my personal journey of loss and shed light on the urgent need for change.

-The Fentanyl Crisis: An Unseen Killer.

Fentanyl, a powerful synthetic opioid, has become a silent killer, responsible for an alarming number of overdose deaths each year. Its potency is staggering, with just a few grains capable of causing fatal respiratory depression. What makes fentanyl particularly dangerous is its prevalence in illegal drug markets, where it is often mixed with other substances, unbeknownst to users. As parents, it is essential to educate ourselves and our teenagers about the risks associated with fentanyl as its use continues to rise among young people.

-Open Border Policies: Fueling the Fire.

The connection between open Southern border policies and the fentanyl crisis cannot be ignored. The lack of stringent border controls has allowed illicit drugs, including fentanyl, to flood our communities. Criminal organizations take advantage of these policies, smuggling drugs across the border, exploiting vulnerable individuals, and fueling addiction. By understanding the impact of these policies, we can advocate for change and demand stronger border security measures to protect our children.

-My Personal Journey of Loss.

In this section, I share my heartbreaking story of losing my son to a fentanyl overdose, highlighting the devastating consequences of the crisis. By recounting the pain, grief, and devastation I experienced, I hope to raise awareness and encourage dialogue among parents and teenagers. It is through these conversations that we can inspire change and prevent further tragedies.

The fight against the fentanyl crisis begins with education, awareness, and advocacy. As parents, we must equip ourselves with knowledge about the signs of addiction, have open conversations with our teenagers, and provide them with support and resources. Additionally, we can actively engage with local and national policymakers to demand effective border control measures and increased funding for prevention and treatment programs.

Conclusion:

The fentanyl crisis is a formidable challenge that demands our attention. By exploring the devastating consequences of fentanyl overdoses and the role our wide-open Southern border plays in perpetuating this crisis, we can work towards a safer future for our children. Let us unite as parents and teenagers, learn from our collective experiences, and strive to transform heartbreak into hope. Together, we can create a world where no parent has to endure the pain of losing their child to a preventable tragedy.

Chapter 6
Open Border Policy

-The Controversy Surrounding Border Policies

In recent years, the issue of border policies has become a topic of heated debate and controversy. For parents and teenagers, understanding the complexities of border policies is crucial to grasp the profound consequences they can have on individuals and communities.

One of the main concerns raised by critics of our open border is the alarming surge in fentanyl overdoses. Fentanyl, a synthetic opioid, has been flooding into the country through illicit channels, claiming countless lives. Many argue that the lax enforcement and porous nature of the wide-open southern border have facilitated the influx of drugs, exacerbating the opioid crisis and leading to the loss of loved ones as my son. The devastating personal account of a parent who lost their child to a fentanyl overdose serves as a powerful reminder of the tragic consequences that can arise from ineffective border policies.

My son serves as a powerful reminder of the human toll these policies can have. Parents, teenagers, and individuals concerned about fentanyl overdoses and the repercussions of the open Southern border must prioritize self-education and actively participate in dialogue with their elected representatives. We desperately need an effective approach to border policies, prioritizing the well-being and safety of all individuals.

-*Examining The Impact of Open Borders.*

Open borders have been a subject of intense debate, with proponents arguing for increased freedom of movement and economic opportunities, while opponents voice concerns over national security and public safety. However, it is crucial to examine the real-life consequences of these policies, especially when it comes to the illicit drug trade.

For many parents, the loss of a child to a fentanyl overdose is a heart-wrenching tragedy that could have been prevented. The Southern border, with its porous nature, has become a gateway for drug cartels to smuggle dangerous substances into our communities. The lack of stringent border control and inadequate resources to combat drug trafficking have contributed to the proliferation of fentanyl, a synthetic opioid responsible for countless deaths.

Examining the impact of open borders also requires considering the broader implications for society. The loss of these young lives not only affects individual families but also has a ripple effect on communities as a whole. It is essential to acknowledge the interconnectedness of our society and the collective responsibility we have in addressing this issue.

My goal is not to vilify immigrants or advocate for closed borders but rather to highlight the need for comprehensive immigration policies that prioritize public safety and protect vulnerable communities.

Together, let us advocate for policies that protect our loved ones from the scourge of fentanyl overdoses caused by the consequences of our open Southern border policies.

-*The Consequences of Inadequate Border Control*

As parents, we have an innate desire to protect our children from harm. We strive to create a safe environment where they can grow and thrive. However, when border control measures fail, our children become vulnerable to the dangers that lie beyond our borders.

One of the most pressing issues we face today is the influx of fentanyl, a synthetic opioid that is wreaking havoc on our communities. This powerful drug, often smuggled into the country through inadequate border control, has claimed countless lives, including that of my beloved son. The consequences of fentanyl overdoses are not limited to one particular demographic or socio-economic group. They affect people from all walks of life, shattering families and leaving communities in despair.

I aim to shed light on the direct link between lax border control policies and the loss of innocent lives. By sharing my personal story and the pain I have endured, I hope to raise awareness among parents and teenagers about the urgency of this issue. It is crucial that we come together as a society to demand stronger border control measures and hold our policymakers accountable for their actions, or lack thereof.

The consequences of inadequate border control are not limited to the loss of life. They extend to the erosion of trust in our institutions and the breakdown of communities. As parents, it is our responsibility to advocate for change and ensure that our children are protected from the devastating consequences caused by our open borders.

Our open border policies have had devastating consequences, contributing to the loss of my 25-year-old son. My mission in writing this book is to ensure that no other parent has to endure the pain my entire family has experienced. We must advocate for stricter regulations and comprehensive drug prevention programs. By doing so, we can protect our children and prevent further tragedy.

Chapter 7

Drug Trafficking Aided by The Open Southern Border

-Unveiling the Drug Trafficking Networks.

I delve into the dark underbelly of drug trafficking and its devastating consequences on our society. Specifically, I shed light on the alarming rise of fentanyl overdoses and how open border policies have contributed to the loss of countless lives, including my own son's.

As parents, it is our responsibility to protect our children from the dangers that lurk in the world. However, the reality is that drug trafficking networks have become increasingly sophisticated, exploiting the vulnerabilities of our communities. Fentanyl, a synthetic opioid that is up to 100 times more potent than morphine, has emerged as a deadly threat, claiming lives at an alarming rate.

One of the key factors behind the surge in fentanyl overdoses is the porous Southern border. This current administration's policies have inadvertently allowed drug cartels to exploit the gaps in security and flood our streets with this lethal substance. The lax enforcement of border controls has provided a fertile ground for criminal organizations to smuggle drugs, including fentanyl, into our neighborhoods.

My personal tragedy serves as a stark reminder of the consequences of these policies. My son, a bright and promising teenager, fell victim to the insidious grip of fentanyl. This poison infiltrated his life through the channels of drug trafficking networks, depriving him of his future and casting our family into a profound and unimaginable grief.

By understanding the complexity of these networks, we can advocate for stricter border controls, ensuring the safety and well-being of our communities.

Moreover, it is essential for parents to have open and honest conversations with their teenagers about the dangers of drug use. By equipping them with knowledge and awareness, we empower them to make informed decisions and resist the allure of substance abuse.

Together, as parents and concerned citizens, we must demand action. We need comprehensive policies that address the root causes of drug trafficking and prioritize the safety of our children. By unveiling the drug trafficking networks and raising awareness about the devastating impact of fentanyl overdoses, we can strive for change and prevent further heartbreak.

Let this be a call to action for parents, teenagers, and all those affected by the scourge of drug trafficking. It is our shared responsibility to protect our loved ones and build a future where hope triumphs over heartbreak.

-The Role of Southern Border States in Drug Transportation.

In the ongoing discourse surrounding border policies, it is crucial to shed light on the significant role that Southern Border States play in drug transportation. This subchapter explores the intricate web of drug trafficking across the border and its devastating consequences, particularly in relation to the fentanyl overdose crisis. By addressing this issue, I hope to provide parents and teenagers with a better understanding of the challenges faced at the border and the urgent need for comprehensive border policies to combat drug transportation.

Understanding the Southern Border States:

The Southern Border States, such as Texas, Arizona, New Mexico, and California, serve as crucial transit points for drug traffickers due to their proximity to Mexico, a major source of illicit drugs. These states bear the brunt of the drug transportation crisis, which has led to an alarming rise in fentanyl overdoses, devastating families and communities alike.

The Fentanyl Overdose Crisis:

Fentanyl, a synthetic opioid, has emerged as a significant contributor to the opioid epidemic in recent years. The ease of manufacturing and its potency have made it an attractive option for drug traffickers. The Southern Border States have become an entry point for fentanyl, resulting in a sharp increase in overdose deaths. It is essential to acknowledge that open border policies play a role in enabling the unchecked flow of drugs, exacerbating the crisis and causing immeasurable loss.

The Loss of a Loved One:

As parents, it is heartbreaking to lose a child to a fentanyl overdose. My personal experiences have led me to advocate for stricter border control measures to curb drug transportation. The loss of my child has become a catalyst for urging policymakers to address the loopholes in the system and prioritize the safety and well-being of our communities.

-The Urgent Need for Comprehensive Border Policies.

To prevent further tragedies, it is imperative to implement comprehensive border policies. These policies should include increased surveillance, enhanced law enforcement collaboration, and technological advancements to detect and intercept drug shipments. Furthermore, investing in drug treatment and prevention programs within our communities is crucial to addressing the root causes of addiction and providing support to those in need. The government can also foster collaboration with neighboring countries and international organizations to create a unified front against drug trafficking. Sharing intelligence, coordinating efforts, and implementing joint operations can enhance effectiveness.

Conclusion:

Understanding the role of Southern Border States in drug transportation is essential in the fight against the fentanyl overdose crisis. By raising awareness and advocating for comprehensive border policies, I hope to prevent further tragedies and protect our children from the devastating consequences of drug trafficking. It is our shared responsibility as parents to demand change and work towards a future where open border policies no longer contribute to the loss of innocent lives.

-The Intersection of Drug Trafficking and Fentanyl Overdoses.

The devastating rise in fentanyl overdoses has become an alarming crisis that demands our immediate attention. As parents and concerned individuals, we cannot afford to turn a blind eye to the dangerous intersection of drug trafficking and fentanyl, as it continues to claim the lives of countless teenagers, young adults and others. In this subchapter, I delve into the heart-wrenching reality of how open border policies have directly contributed to the loss of our children.

Fentanyl, this synthetic opioid that is 50 times more potent than heroin and 100 times more potent than morphine, has rapidly infiltrated our communities, leading to an unprecedented surge in overdose deaths. It is crucial to understand the role that drug trafficking plays in this lethal equation. With the Southern border remaining porous and vulnerable due to misguided policies, criminal organizations have exploited this weakness.

These drug cartels capitalize on the lack of border security, utilizing sophisticated smuggling techniques to transport massive quantities of fentanyl into our country. Their operations are ruthless, showing no regard for human life as they flood our streets with this deadly substance. The consequences are dire, as unsuspecting teenagers fall victim to fentanyl-laced drugs, often with fatal outcomes.

Through my personal experience and research, I have discovered the devastating connection between open border policies and the loss of my son. The unrestricted flow of drugs into our communities has created an environment where fentanyl overdoses have become tragically common. Our children, who should be filled with hope and dreams, are being snatched away from us by an epidemic that could have been prevented.

This subchapter aims to shed light on the stark reality of how open border policies have failed our children and perpetuated the fentanyl crisis. It serves as a wake-up call to parents and teenagers, urging them to recognize the dangers lurking within our communities. By understanding the connection between drug trafficking and fentanyl overdoses, we can begin to address the root causes and advocate for change.

We must advocate for more robust border controls, collaborate on intensified law enforcement initiatives and implement thorough drug education programs to secure our children's future. By uniting our efforts, we can transform heartbreak into hope, ensuring that no parent has to endure the unimaginable pain of losing a child to a preventable tragedy. Let us join hands and fight to protect our loved ones from the devastating consequences of drug trafficking and fentanyl overdoses.

Chapter 8
A Call to Action

-Empowering Parents to Protect Their Children.

In this subchapter, I address the crucial topic of empowering parents to protect their children, particularly in the context of the heart-wrenching consequences of having open border policies and the devastating impact they have had on families. This chapter aims to provide valuable insights and actionable advice to parents and teenagers, especially those who have been affected by fentanyl overdoses and have witnessed firsthand the repercussions of open border policies.

The loss of a child is an unimaginable tragedy, and no parent should have to experience this pain. However, it is our responsibility to equip parents with the knowledge and tools they need to safeguard their children against the dangers associated with fentanyl and other illicit substances.

First and foremost, open communication is key. Establishing a trusting relationship with your children is vital in order to understand their struggles, concerns, and aspirations. Encouraging an open dialogue about the risks of drug abuse, particularly fentanyl, is crucial. Inform them about the potential consequences, emphasizing the life-threatening nature of this potent opioid. By fostering a safe environment for discussion, parents can empower their children to make informed decisions.

Education is another fundamental aspect of protecting your child. Stay up-to-date on the latest information regarding fentanyl, its sources, and the signs of abuse. Educate yourself about the dangers and communicate these details to your teenager. Knowledge is power, and by arming yourself with accurate information, you can help your child steer clear of potentially lethal situations.

Additionally, it is important to be aware of your child's social circle. Encourage them to surround themselves with positive influences and to choose friends who share their values and aspirations. Teach them the importance of setting boundaries and saying no to peer pressure, emphasizing that their well-being is always their top priority.

Lastly, be vigilant about the policies and decisions made by lawmakers regarding open border policies. Advocate for stricter border controls and increased efforts to combat drug trafficking. By joining forces with other affected parents, you can raise awareness and push for change that will prevent more families from enduring the same heartbreak.

In conclusion, empowering parents to protect their children is of utmost importance, particularly in light of the devastating consequences of fentanyl overdoses and the impact of our open Southern border policies, contributing to thousands of overdoses. By fostering open communication, providing education, monitoring social circles, and advocating for change, parents can play an active role in safeguarding their children's well-being.

Chapter 9

Healing and Moving Forward

-*The Journey of Healing.*

In the face of heartbreak and unimaginable loss, the journey of healing begins. For parents who have experienced the unbearable pain of losing a child to a fentanyl overdose, this chapter offers solace and guidance. It acknowledges the profound grief and emptiness that consumes their lives, as well as the guilt and anger that often accompany such a loss. It reassures them that they are not alone and that there are others who understand their pain and are willing to walk alongside them on their journey.

Teenagers, too, can find solace within these pages. They may have witnessed the harrowing consequences of fentanyl overdoses within their own communities, or perhaps they have been tempted by the allure of drugs themselves. Through the stories of parents who have experienced the worst outcome, they can gain a deeper understanding of the dangers and consequences of substance abuse. They can recognize the importance of making informed choices and seeking help when needed.

-Supporting Other Families Affected by Fentanyl Overdoses.

It is important to support families who have been impacted by fentanyl overdoses. The devastating consequences of fentanyl abuse have affected countless lives, leaving behind a trail of heartbreak and despair. As parents ourselves, we understand the immense pain and loss that families endure. By sharing our experiences and empowering others with knowledge and resources, I hope to provide a ray of hope and support for those who are navigating the aftermath of fentanyl overdoses.

-Understanding the Impact.

Fentanyl overdoses have become an epidemic, cutting across all demographics and regions. It is essential for parents and teenagers to gain a comprehensive understanding of this crisis, including the dangers, signs of abuse, and available resources. By educating ourselves and our loved ones, we can work towards prevention and early intervention.

-Supporting Grieving Families.

The loss of a child to a fentanyl overdose is a tragedy no parent should ever have to endure. We must come together as a community to offer support and understanding to these grieving families. By creating safe spaces for open conversations and sharing our stories, we can foster healing and let these families know that they are not alone in their pain.

-Access to Mental Health Services.

The emotional toll of losing a loved one to a fentanyl overdose can be overwhelming. Parents and teenagers affected by this crisis must have access to mental health services that can provide guidance and support during their healing journey. It is crucial to raise awareness about available resources and encourage those affected to seek professional help when needed.

-Advocacy and Policy Change.

While supporting individual families is vital, we must also work towards broader change. Effective and enforceable border policies play a significant role in the availability of fentanyl and other drugs. By advocating for stricter border control measures, we can reduce the inflow of dangerous substances and prevent more families from experiencing the devastation of fentanyl overdoses.

-Building A Support Network.

Parents and teenagers affected by fentanyl overdoses need a strong support network to lean on during their recovery. Connecting with local support groups, community organizations, and online forums can provide a sense of belonging and understanding. By sharing experiences, resources, and coping strategies, we can uplift each other and navigate the challenging path from heartbreak to hope together.

Conclusion:

Supporting families affected by fentanyl overdoses is a crucial step in addressing this devastating crisis. By understanding the impact, offering emotional support, advocating for policy change, and building strong support networks, we can help these families find hope amidst their grief. Together, we can create a compassionate and informed community that stands up against the tragic consequences of fentanyl abuse.

-Embracing Hope and Rebuilding Lives.

Losing a child to a fentanyl overdose is an unimaginable nightmare that no parent should have to endure. However, through our shared experiences and collective strength, we can begin to rebuild our lives and find hope amidst the heartbreak. This chapter is dedicated to helping parents navigate the complex emotions that arise from such a loss and find the resilience to move forward.

I understand that the pain and anger may be directed towards border policies, and it is important to acknowledge the role they played in this tragedy. By shedding light on the consequences of open border policies, I hope to inspire meaningful conversations about the need for change and the importance of securing our borders to protect our children. I emphasize that this discussion is not meant to perpetuate blame or hatred but to raise awareness and advocate for effective policies that would prioritize the safety and well-being of our communities.

Amidst the darkness, we find hope. For parents and teenagers to cope with grief, offering support through counseling, community engagement, and fostering connections with others who have experienced similar losses. I emphasize the importance of seeking professional help to navigate the complex emotions that arise from such a tragic event. Through stories of resilience and healing, I aim to inspire those who feel lost and broken to find strength and hope in rebuilding their lives.

While the pain may never fully dissipate, I believe that together, we can create a world where no parent has to experience the unbearable loss of a child due to fentanyl overdoses. By embracing hope and rebuilding our lives, we honor the memories of our children and work towards preventing similar tragedies from occurring in the future.

-Conclusion: Journey of Resilience and Change.

We have explored the devastating impact of our border policies on families and communities. This journey has been one of resilience and change as I strive to bring light to the heartbreak caused by fentanyl overdoses and the consequences of open border policies.

For parents, this book serves as a wake-up call and a plea to take action. The tragic loss of our children should not be in vain. We must come together, united in our grief, to demand change. It is time to hold policymakers accountable for the consequences of their decisions. Through our collective voices, we can push for stricter border controls, improved drug detection measures, and better support for those struggling with addiction.

Teenagers, too, play a vital role in this journey. You are the future, and your understanding of the issues at hand is crucial. By engaging in open conversations about the dangers of fentanyl and the impact of open border policies, we can educate and empower one another. Together, we can challenge the status quo and work towards a safer and more compassionate society.

To those affected by fentanyl overdoses, I understand your pain firsthand; I share your grief. But amid the heartbreak, there is hope. By sharing my story, I shed light on the reality of this crisis. I aim to break down the stigma surrounding addiction and encourage others to seek help. Together, we can create a support network that saves lives and offers hope for a brighter future.

In conclusion, the Loss of my son Alec is both a call to action and a testament to the strength of the human spirit. It is through our resilience and determination that we can bring about change. Together, as parents and advocates, we can transform heartbreak into hope and create a safer, more compassionate world for all.

The end

About the Author

Armando Fuentes, with over 30 years of experience as a decorated police detective and international banking executive, brings a unique perspective to his writing. Honored as the "1989 Detective of the Year" in South Florida and involved in various federal task forces, Armando has an extensive background in combating organized crime and overseeing complex financial investigations across the Americas.

His book emerges from a blend of professional insight and personal tragedy. Armando's harrowing journey of losing Alec to a fentanyl overdose offers a poignant narrative that connects his law enforcement background to the urgent issue of drug trafficking and its impacts on families. Through his writing, he aims to educate and drive change, hoping to safeguard future generations from similar heartbreak.

Printed in the USA
CPSIA information can be obtained
at www.ICGtesting.com
LVHW020756080224
771080LV00016B/1099